W9-AEZ-132

ALGERIA

A L G

THE REALITIES:

Translated from the French by

E R I A

by *Germaine Tillion*

RONALD MATTHEWS

ALFRED·A·KNOPF *New York* 1958

L. C. Catalog card number: 58–10980

THIS IS A BORZOI BOOK,

PUBLISHED BY ALFRED A. KNOPF, INC.

FIRST AMERICAN EDITION

Originally published in France as L'ALGERIE EN 1957.

My Dear Friends,

FOR several months now, some of you have been asking me to tell you about the Algerian problem. I cannot, however, do this with any brevity, for in fact a whole series of problems is involved. Each of them could be solved—not, indeed, easily or quickly, but solved all the same. Unfortunately, each solution rules out all the others, without, however, affecting the problems that they were designed to solve. This fundamental complexity of the facts is made even more confusing by the amount of falsehoods and false analogies, bad faith, and, above all, ignorance that has beclouded the discussion.

Day by day a flood of downright—and downright contradictory—opinions pours from the French press. The images flash past: Nationalism, Federalism, Separatism, Colonialism, Terrorism, Fatalism, Fanaticism, Communism, Elections, Integration, Negotiations, Capitulation, All-That-France-Has-Done-in-Algeria, All-That-France-Hasn't-Done-in-Algeria, the F.L.N., the M.N.A., the Arab League, the Intelligence Service, the International Petrol Companies, the Holy War. It is a fantastic farrago, rather as if a careless publisher had got hold of the proofs of three or four paper-back thrillers and got them mixed up before sending them to be bound.

You therefore find yourself—like everyone else—a prey to emotional reactions. As far as we former members of the Resistance are concerned—and I am confident I am speaking for most of us—our "conditioned reflexes" are a passionate love of justice, an almost instinctive fellow feeling for the oppressed, the prisoner, and the fugitive, as well as a deep loyalty to our country when it is attacked and when it is in danger.

There are duties that are simple—cruel but simple. Our duty presented itself to us, fifteen years ago, in just that form. Nothing is less "simple" than the struggle we are faced with today, and you can be certain that there is no one for whom it is "simple," except for a few featherbrains—who are pretty evenly distributed on either side of all the world's frontiers. But outside of these people, there is not an actor in the tragedy who is not torn between the most contradictory choices, whether he be in the *fellagha* camps or in our own. I use the word "camps" in the plural, for there is no more unanimity on one side than on the other.

There is one point, however, on which all Algerian Nationalists are agreed. It is that someday, one way or another, they will have to work together with France, though they probably do not realize that for Algeria this collaboration is absolutely vital, even more than it is for Morocco or Tunisia. All the French people I have talked to are agreed, for their part, on another point. It is the debt we owe the Algerians, because they have shed their blood for us in three successive wars, and because they have shared our national lot for 130 years—longer than the inhabitants of Nice and Savoy. I should be inclined to add: because we have involuntarily and unwittingly contributed, by unconscious bad turns and clumsy good turns, to landing them in the blind alley where they are today.

To tell the truth, it is only part of our national lot that they have shared. For, though they have always loyally stood by us in our hours of peril, they have almost always—or, at least, more often than not—been excluded from our successes and our good fortunes, and that is certainly the principal cause of the present tragedy. I have often stated the facts when French people have questioned me. But half the time the person to whom I talked would interrupt me vigorously with: "*But it's their fault. If we'd been in their shoes . . .*" and so on. Then with just as much conviction and equal good faith, the next person I met would cut me short with: "*It's France's fault. All we had to do was to . . .*" and so forth.

You must not expect me to provide you with a ready-made scapegoat that you can blame for everything, nor with a simple and sweeping remedy, despite the enormous choice that is being offered to us. In the Algerian tragedy, as I see it, there are a lot of victims but few criminals—and its possible solutions seem to me to contain the germs of yet further tragedies.

CONTENTS

ALGERIA

I

The Algerian Tragedy

ALGERIA is as impoverished as it is immense, and there are enormous disparities in the people's level of development. The inhabitants number between nine and ten million, of whom the majority (just over eight million) subscribe to the Moslem religion, whereas the rest (just over one million) do not. Finally, with its outdated methods of cultivation, the country is capable of feeding between two and three million people.

The Moslems are often called "natives," but that word grates on me. Nobody in France calls me a "native," though in my own country I am as "native" as can be and devoted to everything, even laughably so, that is most antiquated among the heirlooms of our national inheritance. Perhaps that is the reason why I have always experienced such a fellow feeling for "natives," and why their old-fashioned ways have always seemed to me not only moving but worthy of respect. However that may be, the word "native" in Algeria is looked on as insulting.

The rest of the inhabitants are called "settlers." The strict meaning of the word is a landowner of European origin. In fact, of the 1,200,000-odd non-Moslems in Algeria, there are exactly 19,700 settlers in this strict sense, of whom 7,432 own less than twenty-five acres and are very badly off, unless they are pensioners, tradespeople, or officials who happen to own plots of land on which they are not dependent for a living. The "real settlers" number about 12,000, of whom 300 are rich and a dozen or so extremely rich: this handful of millionaires probably have more money among them than all the rest put together. With their families, the 12,000 settlers form a group of about 45,000 people, for the average European family in Algeria numbers 3.6 persons. The rest of the "settlers"—well over a million men, women, and children—are skilled workers, government officials, office employees, taxi-drivers, garage proprietors, station-masters, nurses, telephone girls, laborers, tradesmen, and heads of businesses; taken together, they probably represent more than three quarters of the economic skeleton of the country, which would not survive their loss. All the same, the word "settler," just like the word "native," is as often as not used in a pejorative sense.

When I talk of the inhabitants of Algeria, I call them Algerians, and I cannot bring myself to run down or to insult either class of them. I understand one as well as the other, and I believe that, for different reasons, we owe a debt to both. Furthermore, "settlers" and "natives" might almost be twins. They have the same good qualities—a sense of honor, physical courage, faithfulness to their word and to their friends, generosity, doggedness—but they also have the same weaknesses—violent dispositions, umbridled love of competition, vanity, suspiciousness, jealousy. These resemblances might be ascribed to the life they have shared for so long, but the curious physical likeness that is also to be found between the two groups calls for another kind of explanation and suggests a glance back at their respective origins.

A high proportion of the "settlers" consists of people who have come from Corsica, Malta, and Spain. Now, the Corsicans are ethnically closer to the Kabyles or the Shaouia of Algeria than they are to the inhabitants of southern France; the Maltese country folk still speak an Arab dialect, and everyone knows what the Spaniards owe to the Moorish blood in their veins.

When it comes to the "natives," we are dealing with people who were born in one of the corners of the globe which, in prehistoric as in historic times, has seen a constant flow of migrant populations, from north to south, from east to west, and from west to east, both on a national scale and an individual family scale. To take an example, the Roman legions who were stationed for centuries in the Constantine area were largely composed of Gaulish soldiers, who brought their families with them, tilled plots of land, and, once they had completed their service, settled down in the country. In fact, if the ghosts of our ancestors, the ancient Gauls, could return to Algeria and take a census of their chromosomes, no one can be quite certain where they would find them. Not that this matters a bit, for no human stock has a monopoly of intelligence and fair-mindedness, and most family trees number among their ancestors a considerable and probably a constant proportion of knaves and fools. We have no reason either to blush or to boast on this score, and I only go into these details because racialist arguments are occasionally used in the Algerian question. I always find such arguments distasteful: here they are stupid as well.

In practice, of course, the idea of race is often confused either with that of language or with that of religion. Algeria is no exception to the rule, and a normal way of classifying a man "racially" is to describe him as a "Moslem" or a "non-Moslem."

It is true, of course, that a man's religious affiliations have an enormous influence on his development. All the same, we must not think of every religion in the world as a vat of dye at once indelible, uniform, and unmistakably identifiable for each faith. I number among my friends a vast number of Moslem men and Moslem women, drawn from almost every level of intelligence and station in society, and I can assure you that a Moslem intellectual, and a practicing Moslem at that, whether he be professor, doctor, lawyer, or teacher, has a religious attitude far closer to that of a Christian intellectual than to that of his illiterate fellow countrymen. And the other way around. In other words, when it comes to religious attitudes, a Breton shepherd has more in common with a shepherd of the Ouarsenis than either of them has with their compatriots who have university degrees. I would go further. If one could dig down below the level of behavior, eliminate the bundle of miscellaneous convictions with which every human being is burdened from his birth, and analyze the real, personal, and living content of people's fundamental religious beliefs, I think it probable that one would find the same resemblance on either side of the frontiers of the faiths. When people talk to you of a "holy war" and of "Moslem fanaticism," don't visualize some sort of innate brutality that does not fit in with the French logic on which we preen ourselves so sickeningly. Just look at a history book and read a little about the contemporaries of Montaigne or even of Descartes, and you will see that the religious hatred that set Catholic Christians and Protestant Christians at each other's throats was blinder, more bloody, more fanatical, and more "innately brutal" than anything that exists today between the Moslem and the Christian communities of Africa. Why? Because fanaticism and ferocity are social facts that depend on the cultural level of a people and not on the nature of its religion. There may be fanatical Moslems (for many poor Moslems have never had an opportunity to learn moderation, or, indeed, to learn at all), but fanaticism is no more an integral part of Islam than the Crusade against the Albigensians or the Witchcraft Trials are essential parts of Christianity. Almost the whole of the world's Moslem population lives in one of the tracts of the globe which has benefited least from the upheaval of the industrial revolution, and all the nonsense that is talked about Islam stems from that.

The level of civilization, however, has a lot to do with behavior, but the business of evaluating it is none too easy, especially where illiterates are concerned; and it is just as hard to analyze the influences to which illiterates have been subjected. Between 1934 and 1940 I spent most of my time on a scientific mission in the Aurès Mountains. In the regions where I stayed the longest, few of the men and none of the women had ever seen a European in their lives. Many of them, on the other hand, had had dealings with Spirits, a subject on which they all, without exception, possessed the fullest and most detailed information.

You would naturally put this down to isolation and a "prelogical" attitude. Yet what struck me most in my own investigations, compared to those which other ethnologists had carried out in the Sudan, in Brazil, in Mexico, and among the Eskimos, was the absence of the exotic. I doubt whether you could put this impression down to a mere kink in my mind (which might be described as more interested in causes and reasons—necessarily of a universal type—than in the picturesque). I am inclined to believe the area came under outside influences in the past, and reciprocated them. Moreover, at the present day the Moslem population of Algeria forms a "conducting medium." And that conductivity is possibly the reason why ideas and opinions borrowed from European civilization can be found in places where European ways have apparently never penetrated. These ideas may have been transmitted, by a sort of social osmosis, from areas where the two communities were in contact.

Fourteen years later the war, the wave of emigration to France, and an economic revolution had insidiously undermined the old traditional institutions and prepared the way for the breakdown into isolated cells which we are witnessing today. Remember that when the next-to-last census was taken, the Moslems in the age group between twenty and sixty numbered 1,600,000. Some of those who were then over fifty had taken part in the 1914-18 war. Those under forty could have been mobilized in 1939, might have been taken prisoner, and might have escaped. Others in the same group—or some of the same men—participated in the liberation of France and the Indochina war. Add to that the contingent of 400,000 men who work in our factories, constantly bringing in over the last ten years fresh blood, and ask yourself what is the percentage in Algeria of adult Moslems who have crossed the Mediterranean. Half? A third? Two thirds? Probably much more in some areas and much less in others. But it is precisely in the areas where they are in the majority that the insurrection came to birth.

These men who worked at Billancourt, at St. Denis, or in the Lorraine blast furnaces; who fought at Verdun, at Charleroi, on the Somme, on the Loire, or at Monte Cassino; who liberated France and crossed the Rhine with De Lattre, have they or have they not emerged from their Middle Ages? They are certainly Moslems, and fervent ones, but they are no more the contemporaries of Sidi Ocba than we are of Saint Louis. No more are they Orientals (the drowsy and poetic Orient, the fanatical and bloody Orient, the resigned and fatalistic Orient, the storied Orient —there is no lack of clichés). Lacking, as they do, education, technical background, and resources, three quarters of them are not Europeans either. What are they, then? They are twentieth-century Algerians —and, believe me, that is not an enviable position. As an old Kabyle used to say, "You've led us to the middle of the ford, and there you've left us."

Some of them, all the same, have made their way across the ford. How many? Maybe as many as a quarter, for one third of the total Algerian population of a little over nine million people lives in a European-type economy and two thirds in an African-type. Which means that most of the European-born minority and about two million of the Moslem majority enjoy a standard of living and of culture comparable to what may be found in France. The rest, six million human beings, all belonging to the majority, have progressively lost the material fruits and the spiritual values of a primitive society. But, at the same time, lack of education and of technical background has prevented them from becoming modern men. They are living on the frontier of two worlds—in the middle of the ford—haunted by the past, fevered with dreams of the future. But it is with their hands empty and their bellies hollow that they are waiting between their phantoms and their fevers.

This kind of despoilment is not a phenomenon peculiar to Algeria. It is affecting, or threatening to affect, three quarters of the human race. But you will more readily understand how it operates and appreciate the injustice and the cruelty if I portray it to you on the scale of a small human community living in the wildest part of the Aurès Mountains—a community in which over a long period of years I knew every man and woman.

In the Middle of the Ford

WHEN I SAW them for the first time, they were all very poor. They always had been. After four or five consecutive years of drought, they might be really up against it, and the authorities occasionally found it necessary to make free distributions of grain. But normally they had enough—just enough—to eat.

Some of them were unhappy. Even in those days I knew of far too many children separated without any reason from their mothers and brought up by a sour stepmother—young people kicked about by their families, and thwarted loves, and irreconcilable hatreds, and a quite fantastic number of murders. But then there is no such thing as a perfect society, and even the best look a lot better if you do not scrutinize them too closely. Private, individual happiness was, I thought, even rarer there than it is among us. On the other hand, in those days I never came across those profound and incurable miseries which are the secret of the great civilizations.

These people had their strong points too—a reasonable chance at a pleasant life, good nature, warm-heartedness, and a sense of humor. Theirs was a fairly well-balanced existence, thanks to the unlimited mutual aid that linked the inhabitants of a village or a group of tents, the pride they all took in this solidarity, the enormous fun they got out of playing dirty tricks on their neighbors and the relative harmlessness of these pranks. I remember particularly the story of two tribes who were traditional enemies and of one of their periodic little wars, which I watched: at the end of three days of uninterrupted fighting, in which everyone had fired to his heart's content, the total of casualties was one man wounded and a sheep killed. Eventually the nearest *marabout* acted as mediator. The victors agreed to compensate the wounded enemy, and everyone got together to make peace and to hush the affair up, not merely from the faraway officials of the Prefecture, but also from the two local

Arab magistrates. But what fun they had had, on both sides!

I said good-by to them in the last week of May 1940. When I saw them again, between December 1954 and March 1955, I was thunderstruck by the change they had undergone in less than fifteen years, and for which the only word I can find is "pauperization." These men who fifteen years before had been living sparingly but reasonably, and in conditions that were more or less the same for everyone, were now split into two unequal groups. In the smaller group, it is true, people were richer than in the old days, but in the other group no one could be sure how he was going to exist between December and June. In the old days, after a good harvest, even the poorest man would put the surplus by for consumption over the next three years, for centuries of experience had taught everyone the need for providence. Now nine families out of ten were living from hand to mouth.

What lay behind it all? There is no lack of explanations, but many of them are not worth the paper they are written on. One classic kind is expressed in such saws as "These people are just shiftless . . . ,"

"They're no more than great big children . . . ," "It's all Moslem fatalism . . . ," and so forth.

A second and no less familiar type of explanation would put the blame for everything on that hoary scapegoat, colonialism. Unfortunately for that argument, there is not and never has been a French settler living nearer than sixty miles. You might, if you liked, blame the sand-laden wind and the goats for the shrinkage of the cultivable lands. But the goats and the wind are not inventions of colonialism.

It is true that by the end of 1954 there *was* a road —though nobody traveled on it except the old-time caravans. There was also a magnificent school—where no teacher had yet been installed. But, as in the old days, one never saw a medical officer or a nurse or, indeed, any sort of official—except, every two or three years, a couple of inoffensive and bewildered gendarmes. In the last month there had been a few soldiers or a few *fellaghas,* but that is another story, or rather another chapter of the same story. "France's contribution" to the country was, to all appearances, conspicuous by its absence: not a single teacher, an empty road, no medical officer, no nurse, no sort of emissary of "civilization." At the most, it had amounted to a few good intentions, which had never been followed up.

The appearances, however, were completely misleading. "France's contribution" was everywhere, invisible but omnipresent, and was distributing good and evil with an open hand. Good and evil, however, as you are going to see, are a little difficult to distinguish here.

True, there are no regular medical rounds, and therefore no periodical distribution of aspirins or lozenges. But malaria, typhus exanthematicus, and typhoid, which were still ravaging the area fifteen years before, have completely disappeared, though the inhabitants may never have seen a white overall or a thermometer. Specialists have marked down the mosquito-infested districts, and DDT has done the rest. In the preceding period, plague and cholera had vanished just as silently, thanks to the same invisible activity of our doctors. Just about the same time, devastating famines and tribal wars, on which the faraway Prefectural administration was keeping an eye, were joining the legends of the past.

You might call it an idyllic picture. There is not a

settler nor an official to be seen, but peace reigns, health has improved, lice are disappearing (with typhus), and mosquitoes (with malaria), and when a real famine does come—not the famine that people groan about, but the famine that kills—high officials come down to superintend the distribution of flour or of rice. Is that all that "colonization" amounts to? Yes, it does sometimes amount to just that, but it is by no means as anodyne and as inoffensive as it might seem.

To put it in a nutshell, the population has shot up; the statistics for Algeria as a whole are now four or five times what they were a hundred years ago. Moreover, the rate of increase has reached a figure which is among the highest in the world, *but which has not yet attained its maximum.* As the people have been multiplying, their flocks and their farms have been expanding in proportion, and have reached and then passed what might be called the danger line, beyond which the soil is irreparably exhausted, springs dry up, and forests vanish once and for all. Thus, while the population is increasing in geometrical progression, natural resources are not only not increasing in arithmetical progression (as Malthus laid down), but have ceased to increase and are even declining.

Meantime, that empty road, on which nobody seemed to be traveling, has opened the way to another type of evolution. The peasants have stopped reckoning in loads of barley and are counting in francs; they have passed almost unawares from a barter economy to a market economy. They have been caught up in the vicious cycle that for centuries had our ancestor, the French peasant of monarchical days, by the throat—the old-time French peasant, with his fecklessness and his sloth and all the vices of the poor, and naturally with his fatalism, which was then, however, called "Christian resignation."

This cycle, which you will find in every undernourished country in the world, starts when the peasant is forced to sell his produce immediately after the harvest in order to pay off his debts—to sell, that is to say, at the bottom price. It continues when five or six months later he is compelled to buy the same produce back at the top price, which means at least double the figure he has given for it. It is easy to see that at this rate the unhappy man gets deeper and deeper into hopeless difficulties. Nevertheless, this cycle, and others like it, are no more than eddies in the vast flood of destitution which today is sweeping whole continents helplessly away with it.

The sudden and unprecedented increase in population, the simultaneous dwindling of resources, the collapse of the economy, and contact with the heartbreaking superiority of foreign techniques are rocking to their foundations the archaic civilizations that have been subjected to this combined offensive. Everything they could boast of is dying or on the point of death: arts, techniques, and all the ingenious devices that permit a human community to live in something like peace. And the process is the essence of logic. Weeks of work and seven fleeces are needed for the weaving of a *burnous*, and each fleece is worth between five hundred and a thousand francs. It is ridiculous for people who eat meat only four times a year to spend all that time and money on a garment when for next to nothing they can get a hand-me-down that may be seedy but will at any rate keep out the cold. It is the same wherever you look, and so in every field the seedy and the sordid are on their way to replacing the splendid survivals of the past.

I am not going to detail the endless series of disasters that the years ahead hold in store for these unfortunate people. Their pastureland? It is over-grazed and exhausted before it can be resown—and the beasts die. The seed corn that embodies their hopes for the coming year? They have been so hunger-stricken that they have eaten it, a handful at a time. They are robbed when they buy. They are robbed when they sell. They will have no more honey, for their bees were killed off in the last drought, and they have not yet restocked their hives. And I have not mentioned the tax-collector, the moneylender, or the insurance collector.

Acts of parliament and officials are powerless to protect poor and illiterate men: a swarm of parasites preys on them. And now there is the rebellion, the *fellagha* and the forces of law and order. And who do you think is caught between the *fellagha* and the forces of law and order? Why, they are. Naturally.

Adapted and Unadapted Peoples

In 1828, when our great-grandfathers crossed the Mediterranean for the operation that was to end in the conquest of Algeria, Algeria was an archaic country. So was France.

The world has changed a bit since then, and the Franco-Prussian War of 1870 was probably the last war of the Middle Ages. My grandfather fought in it. That means that the Middle Ages are still on our doorstep, and that we can make some attempt to understand the men of our own day who have not yet emerged from them.

The new era did not begin with the splitting of the atom, which is no more than an event in its history, but with the enormous development of mechanization, the huge expansion in trade and the increased speed of transport, and, above all, with the great medical discoveries. Along with these phenomena went universal education, the increase of technical skill, and a regular increase in wealth.

All this—the *world-wide* stamping out of epidemics, the *world-wide* commercialization of resources, the *world-wide* dissemination of ideas, discoveries, and news—has resulted in the transforming of the human biological environment all over the world.

Now, part of mankind has adapted itself to the new environment and has gained handsomely from it. The rest of the people did not succeed in adapting themselves at once, and thus started to fall behind, and so every year it is becoming a little harder for them to catch up with their rivals. One of the symptoms of this backwardness is an extravagant increase in population. That is the reason why many people, particularly in Anglo-Saxon countries, have taken the effect for the cause and recommend birth-control as a solution for these unhappy peoples' plight. To preach birth-control to an underdeveloped country is a joke whose cruelty I will try to show you.

The unadapted peoples are living in archaic agricultural civilizations; the adapted peoples in civilizations of the industrial type, their eyes firmly fixed on the future. I have no wish to pronounce any judgment of value between the two. Individually, men are neither less intelligent nor less good and certainly not less happy in a so-called "backward" society than in our own—so long, at least, as no one has tampered with the centuries-old empirical balance that has allowed man to gain a living in that society. There was a time—not so distant, either, for it ended only about 1920—when the two civilizations existed side by side in our own country.

Each of the two civilizations has its own individual type of birth rate, which is tied up with the sum of social demands of the society concerned. To preach biological fertility to people with a Paris, New York, or Moscow university background is no more ridiculous than to call for birth-control among an archaic people, and vice versa. On the other hand, as soon as the two societies come into contact, they tend to have the same type of death rate. The result, for the archaic communities, is a sudden and extravagant increase in their population.

The two civilizations not only have different types

of birth rate. In the economic field, they display fundamentally different types of productivity.

In archaic societies, where human reproduction rates are at the maximum, resources remain more or less stationary. With good luck they may increase a little, but they tend to diminish once they have reached a ceiling, which they soon attain. The inevitable result of this simultaneous growth of population and diminution of resources is a constant, tragic, progressive, and inexorable fall in the standard of living.

In industrial civilizations, on the other hand, the increase of wealth is swift and, as far as one can judge, without any limit, while the figure of the population changes little and sometimes does not even change enough. The result, of course, is the exact opposite of the trend in archaic societies, and we see a constant and substantial rise in the general conditions of the population's existence.

This is no argument for or against Malthusianism. Theoretically, people should be anti-Malthusian in Malthusian societies and Malthusian in the archaic environments where it is impossible to be so. One has only to state the problem in these terms to show the absurdity of hoping for a ready-made solution: each civilization forms a homogeneous whole that cannot be marketed in interchangeable separate parts. It is like a vintage car: when one of the parts is worn out, the only answer is to get a new vehicle.

Increase in wealth and increase in population are therefore two distinct phenomena, and their appearance in the two systems is always out of step: in the new civilizations wealth is increasing, but not population; in the old, it is the population that is increasing, but not the wealth. And when the mean individual income in each sector is worked out, it will be seen that the standard of living is falling faster in the so-called underdeveloped countries than it is rising in the modern ones. In fact, the position is even worse than the statistics would indicate, for figures can only show—more or less accurately—the sum of individual incomes and the number of men who have to share them; but they can give no information about how the first is distributed among the second. Now, as soon as the economy of an archaic country begins to collapse, a parasitic class comes into being which corners an increasing share of the national income and of whatever foreign investments there may be.

Their digestion of these only whets the parasites' appetite for the absorption of the other resources of the country. And one finds oneself asking whether, when the poverty and the ignorance of a people drop below a certain level, investments do not add to the impoverishment, just as the cultural destitution is aggravated by the "fight against illiteracy" which the international cultural institutions are forever prating about.

The result of this double process is that part of the world's population (about a quarter) is growing steadily richer, whereas three quarters of mankind (and it will soon be more) is on the slippery slope of a growing impoverishment for which the only word I have been able to find is pauperization.

In areas where huge tracts of virgin land make it possible temporarily to stave off overpopulation, archaic communities do survive which are as yet neither adapted nor pauperized. But obviously this is only a stay of execution, whose duration one can almost predict by comparing the figure of the community's population with the number of square miles of utilizable land it has at its disposal. Ethnographers should hurry up and have a look at them, for in a little while it will be too late. And while we are about it, let us spare a moment to regret their carved masks, their carpets, their embroidered *jellabas,* so soon to disappear before the invasion of blue overalls, or rags. For my part, I shall shed a tear over their misery—for there is room for tears.

I should say that the greatest crime of the eighteenth century was the slave trade, and I should call colonialism the corresponding crime of the nineteenth century. But the crime of our age is going to be the pauperization of three quarters of the human race, which is in full cry at the moment all over the world. What about the concentration-camp system? you will say. That can probably be regarded as an extreme rationalization of the phenomenon, an attempt to make it a paying proposition.

The anti-slavery drive was the alibi of colonialism (it still is, occasionally), and I wonder whether anti-colonialism is not on the way to becoming the alibi of pauperization. Not that colonialism is completely dead—it is merely dying—or that it has not worsened the economic position of the countries which have had to endure it. But it is not solely to blame for their poverty; at the present moment, for instance, undernutrition in the parts of Algeria where there have never been settlers seems more of a threat to the poor than it is in the areas where settlers abound. For the colonizing settler is to the colonized population rather what insulin is to the diabetic, at once a sign of his illness and a temporary palliative. To cut the insulin off before the diabetes has been cured is to kill the patient; to assert that good health consists in taking insulin would be to snap one's fingers at the world.

IV

The Solution of the Problems of the Unadapted Peoples Calls for a Genuine Social Mutation

IN THE COUNTRIES that have had the incredible luck to catch the train in the nick of time—the express of world civilization—adaptation has taken place insensibly, so that few people realize what a revolutionary process it has been.

Today, in these countries, there is not a child who does not come under the attention of a cohort of doctors, even before he is born. After his birth his lungs, heart, eyes, and teeth are checked regularly. His feeding has developed into a science that is making constant progress; he is obliged to undergo many years of education; in a word, he benefits from all the care and protection at the disposal of the country that he has done the honor of choosing for his own. And it is only right that all this should be done for him, for to his country he represents a guarantee of future strength and continued progress, and thus of independence and prosperity. But he can only be such an asset if he is looked after properly, and that fact must be borne well in mind.

Thus, every child is ushered along a continuous moving stairway to the age when he will specialize and choose a trade. With every year that goes by, in the adapted countries, specialization imposes more demands and trades become more complicated, but at the same time the social dividend becomes greater. One child turns into a skilled workman or a surgeon, another into a salesman, an atomic physicist, or a minister—it matters little which, for the foreman's son will become a politician or a scientist if he wants to or if he sees the opportunity.

This being so, every child who comes into the world calls for more and more care and expense from his parents and has more and more chances of escaping illness. Simultaneously with this evolution, however, fewer and fewer children are being born, so much so that the state must see that the birth rate does not decline too far, thus obliging it to offer yet further protection to the child and the family. For in modern countries, normal men and women realize the serious injury they would be causing their child if they did not see to it that he got good and plentiful food, scrupulous medical attention, as long an education as he needs, a certain standard of general comfort—clothing, good air, games, and holidays—and, finally, a trade. All these advantages do not constitute a privilege: on the contrary, it is a serious handicap to be deprived of them. Now, even if a married couple were to deny themselves everything, they could not shoulder this burden for the "annual child" that corresponds to the biological rhythm of human reproduction.[1]

---

[1] In French Canada, even though the birth rate is limited both by monogamy and by the prohibition of divorce, women with more than twenty living children are by no means uncommon. There is on record the case of a woman who had never once had occasion to menstruate in the whole course of her life; she had been married young, and then had been pregnant without interruption up to the menopause. But Canada has the area of Europe and the population of Belgium, and it can afford to combine, in certain areas, a productivity of the industrial type with an archaic-type birth rate.

In a country such as Algeria, social customs are among the most favorable in the world to a maximum reproduction rate:

It is not merely egotism that makes modern peoples limit their births; much more often it is parental love —in other words, the same law of the preservation of the species which makes archaic people do precisely the opposite. And two attitudes that appear to

---

marriage takes place very early, and repudiation of a wife by her husband is easy and frequent. Unless, therefore, an "economic mutation" occurs, there is reason to expect an increase in the birth rate even bigger than the statistics would suggest. And according to the statistics, the Algerian population is going to double every twenty years, and will reach twenty million inhabitants in 1975 and forty million in 1995.

The statistics, indeed, permit no more than an incomplete empirical prediction of demographic developments, for they record indiscriminately contradictory phenomena, the existence of which we occasionally do not even see. Thus, the biological shock that Algeria has undergone has had two diametrically opposed consequences in the demographic field: above a certain level of income and culture, the birth rate drops; below that level, it rises. Ethnographical inquiry reveals the existence of the two phenomena, often in the same environment, but statistics give us no clue to the real extent of one or the other. *If Algeria's progress in such things as education and the standard of living were to be slowed down or stopped, I think it probable that the increase in the birth rate would exceed even the enormous figures of current predictions.* In the other eventuality, with universal education and a substantial raise in pay for wage-earners as a whole, a generation would see the Algerian birth rate approximating that of Western Europe.

be diametrically opposed probably produce much the same result in the two peoples: a relatively stable population.

If an archaic community is to survive, it must bring into the world as many children as possible, and even so it will be at the mercy of an epidemic, a lost battle, or a year of exceptional drought. It is obvious to anyone who has ever studied a community of this type that all its collective sentiments and all its institutions are such as to promote a maximum rate of reproduction, and it is equally obvious that things could not be otherwise.

When an archaic community comes into contact with technical civilization, the stamping out of epidemics slashes its death rate. But that is not the only effect on its demography, for as the death rate is falling, the birth rate is rising, owing to the antibiotics that put an end to cases of sterility of gonorrheal origin and abortions due to syphilis. The number of the latter is such that in many tribes in Algeria, penicillin is known as "the drug that brings children." [2] Simul-

---

[2] A doctor in Indochina has made a fortune merely by giving a shot of penicillin to all his pregnant patients.

taneously, social causes are working to the same end, for the intensification of trade, the weakening of tribal ties, and the increase in the population are breaking up or enlarging the inbreeding clans that, a bare few years ago, permitted marriage only between cousins. Whether the clans grow bigger or break up, the result is the same: it becomes easier to marry, and the number of births rises. The simultaneous fall in the death rate and rise in the birth rate make for a staggering increase—in geometrical progression—of the population. The ever growing number of men naturally try to increase their flocks and the area of their fields, to be able to live. This results in a progressive destruction of soil, springs, and forests, and a concomitant shrinkage in the population's resources—for which the few technical improvements provide little if any compensation. Chronic malnutrition sets in, and it seems that this too stimulates the birth rate.

But you must not imagine that this appalling prospect provides an archaic population with any reason for limiting births, for it is we who see the prospect, and not they. For them, nothing has changed, at least on the surface. Why should they throw overboard the sentiments they have built up through thousands of years of adversity during which each little group, threatened by thousands of perils, was constantly in danger of extinction? Those sentiments are the most vital and the most treasured possession in their heritage, and, in any case, such people do not have at their disposal some alternate ideal or a spare morality, for no one has thought of giving them one. The material background of their lives has not changed either: the children grow up on their own, as they always have, among the chickens and the goats. And, as in the past, they have as many babies as they can; when a couple does happen to be childless, man and wife feel it so much that they will go to consult the foreign doctor—the doctor who, in countries where overpopulation is a tragedy, will never find patients asking him how to limit their families. All this is perfectly coherent, and only shows that there is no human problem which is purely physiological, and that in this problem, the most serious of all, the physical, the psychological, and the social are all working together to the same end.[3] So it is more and more rare to find meat in the

---

[3] In Kabylia, where inheritance of house property is confined strictly to the male heirs, a woman who has no son or a girl

stew, and the scrap of cake will contain more and more bran or even acorn flour. Hunger has become an everyday sensation, but in the old days people sometimes died of it, whereas now the cruel kindness of the civilized countries keeps the little flame of life alight, though it is sinking lower and lower.

One day the ground which has been handed down for cultivation from father to son—and which is now shrinking with every generation—is not able to support the family, even poorly, even on the lowest standards. The day of pauperization has come.

The pauper has even less reason than the "archaic man" to worry about his offspring, for he has nothing to leave them except his poverty, his dreary hopelessness, and his irresponsibility. And where can he find the courage to be ambitious for his children when they have not the smallest chance of escaping from the frightful, the inexorable clutch of this penury which is rising, insensibly, like a flood?

For the future is going to be even darker than the

---

who has no brother can be turned out of her husband's or her father's house on his death. It is therefore a disaster for a woman not to have a son, and if she happens to have daughters whom she loves, the disaster is even worse.

present, and one has only to consider the improvements in the lot of the so-called underdeveloped countries in the true light of their unhappy populations to realize the completeness of their futility. Everything that has been said, written, or done in this area up to now has been either ineffectual or downright harmful. For there has been nothing to give us hope that the peoples concerned will enjoy the improvements that are being talked about, nor even that there will be a halt in their descent into the abyss of destitution; those who have fallen into this abyss always believe they have reached its bottom, but it is in reality bottomless.

Most of our newspapers—especially when there is a shortage of hard news—like to paint for their readers a complacent picture of the bountiful future that contemporary science holds in store for us. And, indeed, for the readers of these papers, there is nothing unreasonable about such predictions, for (as the Gospel says in slightly different terms) he who has a bicycle will one day have a car, and he who has an icebox can hope to get a refrigerator. But from him who has nothing, there will be taken even that which he thinks he has.

ALGERIA

. . . .

I have never been able to keep my temper when I read glowing stories about the prospects held out by Chlorella—an edible seaweed that will be available at an infinitesimal cost. I am convinced that in fifty years' time the poorest of Frenchmen will be getting as much as he likes of dishes a lot more delicious, and will not give a damn for Chlorella. As for the others, the people without schools, without land, without a trade, the people whose numbers are doubling every twenty years (but with Chlorella they will triple), try and picture their future fate, squatting on their dung between the free distribution—it will have to be free —of Chlorella and of DDT. Think of the unhappy children proliferating in this penury and this humiliation. We at least in our concentration camps had a past to look back on, a past of dignity, of useful work, of thought and responsibility, and this memory enabled most of us, until the final agony, to remain members of the human race.

With or without Chlorella—which is only a symbol —no country in the world can today afford not to provide each individual with a school and a trade. It is a complete mistake to think that the threats to the existence of the so-called underdeveloped peoples are concerned exclusively with food or with population, and that simple little dodges like birth-control, Fundamental Education, or Chlorella will suffice to cope with the problems. On the contrary, what makes the problems so difficult is that they can be solved only by the people involved changing over from one system to another—*that is to say, by nothing less than a mutation.* Such a mutation demands that every individual concerned adopt an ideal of life completely different from the one still set before him by the society in which he lives. Furthermore, it calls for sacrifices, intense and unremitting work, and discipline, based on hope. There are learned folk who will tell you that, for some mysterious reason, certain kinds of people are incapable of work, ambition, and discipline. I doubt this very much. On the other hand, it is obvious that they have not really got the slightest chance of attaining the ideal of life which has been proposed to them, and that in their case *the reasonable solution*—the solution we should adopt if we were in their shoes—is black resignation, or unconditional revolt: there are no other alternatives in the world they are offered.

A journalist writing a series of articles on the Middle East talks of the "pathological hatred" that the people there feel for everything Western. An ethnologist, speaking of the Indians of Brazil, deplores the deep-rooted feelings of hatred, suspicion, and despair aroused in them by everything pertaining to our systems. But surely it is only natural. Like fairy gold, everything we give them turns into dry leaves in their hands. This impotent and despairing hatred is the only refuge of men who cannot even revolt against the gangrenous filth that our civilization becomes by the time it reaches them. The panting locomotive that inspired Honegger to write *Pacific 231* turns into the rusty old sewing-machine that is ruining their embroiderers. Our philosophers, our historians, and our scientists have shrunk to a lout's asinine guffaw at all these men revere.

The reaction of revolt is midway between that of hopeless despair (that of the American Indians and the Arabs of the Middle East) and the balanced attitude of those whom circumstances allow to feel some hope for the future. Algeria is today midway between the two extremes, but it would take only a hair's weight to tip the balance one way or the other and to settle her fate.

The *Sine Qua Non* of Any Possible Mutation

A big, rapid, and general increase in wealth and in education is an indispensable condition for the social mutation that alone can save these peoples today. But it calls for a prodigious effort. A few figures, which represent the most conservative estimate, will give some idea of what is involved:

Elementary education (from six to fourteen), per child: 300,000 francs[1]
One year's vocational training, per adolescent: 600,000 francs

---

[1] At the exchange rate of early 1958, one dollar equaled approximately 400 francs.

Investment necessary to provide each job in industry: 3,000,000 or 4,000,000 francs
A worker's dwelling: 1,000,000 francs

The strain of such an expenditure, big though it is, can be borne by a country in the position of having only to maintain its current standard of living. But for an archaic country or, worse still, a country that has already been pauperized, can you imagine the terrifying sacrifices required if it is to save the entire population on this basis? And yet do you really believe that a people can be saved at any lesser price?

Do not think that you can do a cut-rate job with a sixth of a ballot paper (as in Algeria),[2] a few tubes of vaccine, a generous distribution of our "surpluses," and the "fight against illiteracy" that UNESCO is always preaching. All these signs of our loving care can have only one result (which, in fact, they do have): the inevitable submersion of the values, techniques, and traditions of the inhabitant, a steady diminution of the country's wealth, and a social distortion that will be all the more explosive because the loving care will have been lavish without ever approaching ade-

[2] See note, page 66.

quacy. In a country where many people can read, it is a sound policy to teach the illiterate, but in one where the majority of the population are sunk in ignorance, the fight against illiteracy may prove to be one more calamity. For a man can live in an archaic system, and he can also live in our system: it matters little whether he is happier in one than in the other, for he will never have the choice, and evolution is a one-way process. But in the "pauper" system, the misery is obvious beyond discussion, and the chances of escaping from it are practically nil. And anyone who knows the facts can see that sooner or later the decline into pauperization I have described will befall any archaic country that does not succeed either in avoiding contact with us or in adapting itself—and by adapting itself I mean *educating all the children* and providing a *trade* and a *job* for all adults. Moreover, a simple calculation will reveal that the number of "men who are biologically adapted" (or who are going to be in the near future) amounts to less than a quarter of the human race, while that of the "paupers" (or of the unfortunates in danger of pauperization) consists of the entire remainder of humanity.

Which are the "biologically adapted" countries?

Those where the standard of living can be counted on to rise continuously; that is to say, the two Big Powers—the United States and the Soviet Union—and a few others—England, France, Belgium, Holland, the Scandinavian countries, Western Germany, Australia, and Canada. Almost all of them shared our luck and were among the leading runners in the race of civilization at the moment when it mattered. I agree that you can find in France, in the Soviet Union, and even in the United States communities which fit in perfectly with the definition of an underdeveloped country, but there is every reason to hope that they will progressively catch up with the more fortunate communities.

On the other hand there are the ill-fated countries, those which have fallen behind, where the bit of daily bread becomes every year a little drier and a little smaller: Saudi Arabia, India, Vietnam, Egypt, part of Tunisia, two thirds of Algeria, certain areas of South and Central America, and parts of Eastern Europe.

Between the heights and the depths there is, of course, a slope; and though it is terribly steep and slippery, there are some countries that are hanging on to it and trying to haul themselves toward the top

—Italy and Portugal and, a little lower down, Spain, Yugoslavia, Poland, Japan, and Hungary. For such nations, the chances of history may be decisive. Some outside aid or a good government, and they are saved; a war, a revolution, a little extravagance or a little foreign exploitation, and they are sunk.

We can get some idea of the colossal difficulties faced by a backward civilization that attempts the vital task of catching up with the leaders of civilization by taking a look at the countries that have gone all out in such an attempt: the Soviet Union and Japan. The first has paid—and what a price: seventeen million dead, including twelve million dead of famine!—for the right to sit down at the head table among the rich. But even at this price the Soviet Union succeeded only thanks to her vast natural resources, an iron discipline, and an industry that even before the First World War was making enormous strides. Japan, despite heroic efforts and an outstandingly industrious and disciplined population, has thus far failed. And now China is throwing herself into the exhausting struggle, her only assets a handful of bad examples to avoid.

I am doing my best to present a short and simple

picture of the problems confronting the old archaic countries that want to survive. I must, however, say a word or two about one problem that seems to me particularly tragic and fundamental: it is that of the balance between town and country—that is to say, between industry and agriculture.

The sensational progress of such countries as the mighty United States, Canada, Australia, and, on its own smaller scale, the tiny State of Israel, was undoubtedly greatly speeded up by the fact that these countries were composed of emigrants and consequently did not have a native peasant class. That fact allowed them to keep their agriculture in step with their industry from the start, and the same fact prevents our learning from their example.

It was not that way with Japan and the Soviet Union, and it looks as if Japan's continued poverty can be imputed to her failure to solve the problems of her rural proletariat. As for the Soviet Union, there are innumerable facts to suggest that agriculture is the most disturbing and the most vulnerable domain of her economy. The terrible famines of the regime's first years, the police rule on a scale and of a duration that appear hard to justify, a surprising decline in the birth rate—all these things can be explained only by the murderously costly experiments with the peasant problem and an unfortunate attempt to do away with the peasants as a class.

The alarming fact is that there has up to now been no example anywhere of success in this field, except in countries where popular education and prosperity go a long way back—Denmark, Holland, and (to a smaller extent) France. *Since the beginning of the twentieth century saw the great bound forward of world civilization, which is sweeping away all the old institutions, not a single peasant people has exchanged poverty for comfort, but only comfort for poverty.* That is a frightening thought.

Supposing (a highly improbable supposition) that all the privileged countries agreed tomorrow to submit to any sacrifice that was necessary in order to depauperize the world, would they have the means to do so? Almost certainly not, to judge by the enormous scale of the effort required. That may help to explain the cruel little square dance in which from time to time the two Big and the two Medium Powers exchange satellites—for when the latter do not get something they want from the Power to which they are attached, they quite naturally (and with just as little success) seek it elsewhere. Can the Soviet Union satisfy the appetite for technicians, machines, and capital of China and Vietnam, Poland, Hungary, and the Balkan countries? Can France provide the equivalent of the advantages she enjoys to all the peoples of the French Union? Can the United States (which has undertaken to save the world, but which has devoted to the Point Four program a mere quarter of what France has distributed in North Africa alone since 1947) hope to accomplish in the countries it is helping anything more than an intermittent sprinkling of benefits which feeds poverty but not the poor? All this sort of thing is about as effective (and is inspired by much the same principles) as the penny that some of us may have received from our parents on Sundays to give to the beggar outside the church door.

It does no more good to accuse the rich countries of meanness than to accuse the poor countries of ingratitude. It is quite true that the money given to the poor countries is of next to no use to them—when it does not make their situation worse. All the same, for the rich countries the money represents a heavy sacrifice.

In France, for instance, it is common knowledge that old workers do not have enough to live on, and that when the government wanted to give them a pitiful pension, it did not know where to turn for the money. In the Soviet Union, the peasants go barefoot. In the rich United States, taxation is crushing, social insurance does not exist, and one does not have to depend on hearsay to know that there are such evils as poverty, hunger, illiteracy, alcoholism, and derelict children. All these countries consider that the aid they give to the underdeveloped peoples represents a big effort, and it is distressing to realize to what an extent this effort is useless and even harmful.

It should be emphasized that everything revolves around the question of proportion. One child in twenty going to school is enough to bankrupt the traditional education the other nineteen get, but if the twenty of them could be accommodated in a modern school, all twenty would be able to stand the blow of modern society. A single industrial plant in an archaic agricultural country is enough to make the fortune of parasitic speculators and to bring the old economy down in ruins, but if enough industries are started to raise the general wage level, the whole country is saved. A few tubes of antibiotics and vaccines will suffice to capsize a centuries-old biological balance, but if the unhappy castaways are given enough schools and factories along with the antibiotics and vaccines, they will become acclimated on another level and they will survive.

Everything that is done for the unadapted countries below the standard I have just described can only hasten their ruin. Unfortunately, as the things that could save them are too expensive, we give them what will sink them.

It would be something if we could only leave them alone. Alas, that too is impossible, for the devil has put into their subsoils temptations that we are incapable of resisting.[3] The unhappy people have every reason to hate us.

---

[3] The United States is proposing to give the Arab countries a special grant of aid *which is designed to cover all these countries, North Africa included, and which may reach a total, over two years, of* $400,000,000. The sum is rather less than half of what France is spending every year on Algeria alone.

Meanwhile, we learn from an official report that of the 500,000 adolescents under fifteen among the only community that is a ward of the United Nations (the Arab refugees from Palestine), 408 received vocational training in the year

1955-6. That is to say, UNWRA is not doing even a quarter of its duty (as France is in Algeria), but only a thousandth part. Not that this should make us feel any better, for the impotence of others should not be used to justify our own.

ALGERIA

France's Good Luck and Algeria's Bad

LET US NOW have a look, from this point of view, at the position of France. It is, of course, a country that is, relatively speaking, favored by nature, but not more than other areas in the world where people are still living today in horrible poverty.

Our first bit of good luck was that we brought off our political revolution and our agrarian revolution about fifty years before the beginning of the industrial age and a good century before the biological revolution. Thus we found ourselves in an advantageous position at the most important moment in the history of the world: the first half of the twentieth century. That is why, despite the blood-letting of 1914 and the disaster of 1940, despite eleven years of world wars and I do not know how many of colonial wars, despite our misfortunes and our stupidities, we can still be called lucky because when the fateful hour struck, we were to be found in the camp of the winners. By that I mean the group of countries where the standard of living is rising regularly. I readily agree that luck was not everything, and that we can also claim good management. But it is not so hard to display good management when one is in a position to make a good thing out of it.

Any one of us can easily check on the progress of this mounting graph of our good fortune without bothering to pore over books or to dig up statistics. All you have to do is to sit down beside a poor peasant or an old workman—it does not matter who he is or from what part of France he comes—get him talking, and listen to him, as I have done myself time and again.

He will tell you about his childhood: to school at six "to get his three R's"; at work as a shepherd by the age of eight—smaller than his own sheep; miserly masters who begrudged him his crust of bread—there was no question of meat or sugar. Later: "they gave us three francs a day, reaping by hand. We worked like slaves. The harvest went on for two months. After that, you could hump the swag"—in other words, go begging. And there was sickness, and there was unemployment, and there was the rent day.

Admittedly, there are still a lot of things wrong in France today—slums, low wages, deserted children, destitute old people—but in every area there is a steady and regular improvement. The same improvement can be seen in all the countries that are on the far side of the dividing-line—not the dividing-line that separates the Communist bloc from the Atlantic bloc, but a quite different line, which has nothing to do with alliances or political programs: the line that divides the bloc of the hungry, who every year are going to get a little hungrier, from the bloc of the well-fed, who are getting richer every year.

Now try going to Algeria—I have just come back from there—and sit down at the door of a *gourbi*, beside the grandfather of the family, as I have done thousands of times. Talk about the last harvest, the state of the grazing, the health of the goats, the price of oil, the price of dates. Then listen, take notes, check and compare.

Two thirds of the Algerian people have experienced

a fate the direct contrary of ours in France. Their misfortune was that they were in the trouble zone of the modern biological revolution *before they had reached the standard of living and of education which I propose to call the "level of self-defense."* And that is where, as I see it, our responsibility comes in.

I say "our responsibility" and not "our fault," for Algeria's present plight was probably inevitable—insofar as it is impossible today to shield an archaic civilization completely from contact with the juggernaut of world civilization, and insofar as such contact is fatal to people who are not prepared. It is equally true, however, that our presence in Algeria has *speeded up* the phenomenon of the social disintegration of the unfortunate country. So, if you prefer, we will say that if Algeria had remained independent, the population would have doubled, whereas with us there it has quadrupled, which considerably worsens Algeria's present position and helps to make it insoluble. But that is an unforeseen and unintentional consequence of our "colonialist paternalism," a consequence for which we can feel both responsible and innocent—as responsible and as innocent as those who are its victims.

Algeria has today a population of nine or ten million; in 1839 it probably had less than two million; the statisticians predict for it (if the economic conditions of 1954 continue) twenty million in twenty years' time and forty million in forty. Which is midsummer madness, for an Algeria which was an autonomous and thus perforce an agricultural country would be able to feed only two or three million—and poorly, at that.

In 1954 the proportion of illiteracy in French among the Moslem population was 94 per cent for men and 98 per cent for women, and one Algerian child in four was going to school. This last figure, however, referred to all Algerian children, girls as well as boys, non-Moslems as well as Moslems. In reality, only one Moslem boy in five was going to school and one Moslem girl in sixteen. Even these disgraceful figures do not tell the whole truth: no statistics do until you analyze them. For in Algeria there was a problem which demanded even more attention than that of "Moslem versus non-Moslem" or "settler versus native": the problem of "town versus country." In the towns, universal education for children of all faiths was within sight—with thirteen out of every eighteen Moslem children at school in the city of Algiers—whereas in the country it remained a mere daydream. In some country districts there is room in the schools for one child in fifty; in others, it is only one in seventy.

People do not miss things they have never heard of, and our ancestors in the Aurignacian caves felt no deprivation at the absence of the radio or of central heating. But there are probably more people in Algeria than in any other country who have a personal and direct knowledge of certain kinds of advantages—education, political rights, modern family relationships, the possibility of rising in the world—which they have no real hope of ever sharing. These advantages, which we take as a mere matter of course, are nothing but frustration for the Algerians, who know what they are missing and feel resentment.

Our newspapers draw complacent comparisons between the Algerian standard of living and that of Egypt or Arabia.[1] It may well be that the people of Algiers or of Constantine are a little better off than

---

[1] Average annual income in Algeria, 54,000 francs; southern Italy, 50,000 francs; Egypt, 40,000 francs; India, 25,000 francs; Yemen, 14,000 francs.

the inhabitants of the Red Sea coast. But the people on the Red Sea coast do not know the meaning of comfort or freedom, or even the simple satisfaction of being able to eat their fill every day. Above all, they do not know that this satisfaction is a common and ordinary thing which whole populations enjoy without ever imagining that they are privileged.

In the same way, it takes a cataclysm such as the one we went through twelve years ago for the citizens of privileged countries such as ours to know from personal experience the shades and gradations of starvation.

There are two sorts of starvation. In primary hunger, the obsession is for a volume of food sufficient to fill the stomach—bread, flour, or rice. In the concentration camps we saw some of our comrades, under the influence of this "primary hunger," wolfing down two or three mess tins of turnips if they were given the rations of sick or dead fellow prisoners. When we sometimes daydreamed among ourselves of the unattainable dishes that haunt the imagination of the famished, one often heard a fellow prisoner naming as his first choice: "Bread to start with, lots and lots of bread."

When the stomach is full, another sort of starvation, "secondary hunger," takes the place of the first. It is a hunger for meat, fats, and fruit, and the more this "secondary hunger" is appeased, the quicker the consumption of bread, potatoes, rice—and turnips—diminishes.

My investigations of family budgets in the Algerian countryside gave me the impression that, *thanks to the emigration of Algerian workers to France,* primary hunger is more or less satisfied in Algeria, for what that is worth. Not, indeed, everywhere, and not for everyone, for, unfortunately, in the weeks before the new harvest is in, some families in Kabylia are reduced to eating acorn biscuits, and in the Aurès Mountains boiled juniper berries. As for "secondary hunger," only the families of the rich (a tenth of the population) and those of industrial workers (100,000 employed locally and 400,000 emigrants in France) can satisfy that. When I used to ask in a *gourbi* in Zaccar or the Ouarsenis how long a load of wheat or barley lasted, the reply I got told me how near the people were to hunger. If the daily consumption was a liter a head, I knew that "primary hunger" had been satisfied, but that "secondary hunger" was always hanging over the unfortunate household. When the consumption of cereals was less, it meant either that the family was comfortably off (a little sugar, a little butter, a little meat, and some milk) or that they were suffering complete penury, the sort of hunger which gives people cramps in the stomach.

One should not forget that every other grown man in Algeria has worked in France. That means that when he sees this poverty before him, he can and does recall memories of a quite different world. He can remember high-spirited, well-washed, well-dressed children who have a good, thick slice of bread with jam waiting for them when they get back from school, busy housewives with their bags stuffed full of the day's groceries, and those warm and cozy kitchens you see through the windows in the evening after the lights have been turned on and before the curtains are drawn.

It is true that the Algerian who is working or has worked in France is an aristocrat by comparison with the rest of his compatriots. His family is not so poorly fed or clothed as his neighbors', and he shares the benefits that the French workers have won, at least as far as wages are concerned, for French legislation stipulates that he shall be paid at the same rate as his French-born fellow worker.

Let us take a closer look, though, at the way this aristocrat lives. On paper, he draws the same wage in France as our own workers, but the French worker lives with his family; as often as not, the Frenchman's wife goes out to work too, and with two paychecks to draw on, the household has a little bit more than is needed for the bare necessities—the "little bit more" that is one of the essentials of a happy existence. When the wife does not work, she runs the house, cooks, washes, sews, irons, does the shopping, and saves some money. . . . In a Moslem worker's family there is only one paycheck, and generally there are twice as many children. It is the husband who runs the house, does the shopping, keeps the accounts, and sews. He looks after the baby when it is ill, and when the mother cannot feed it, the father sometimes gives it the bottle. I have known men in various walks of life who had patiently passed on to their wives a few of the crumbs of civilization they had picked up on their travels, but they were outstanding people; the others—the majority—just give up. I remember one little official, all of whose children had trachoma, talking to a fellow Moslem who was giving him some advice about hygiene. "You know perfectly well that we've all married sluts," the little official said.

You may say that perhaps the women do not know there is any other way of living. But they do. In the towns they go to the movies now, they listen to the radio, either at home or at a neighbor's, they gossip among themselves, they get to know things, and even in villages out in the back of beyond I heard remarks of an astonishing bitterness last year. They know that it is easier in their country to get rid of a good honest wife and to separate her once and for all from her children than it is in ours to fire a servant.

The forcing of women into marriage; the legal sale of little girls to old men; polygamy; the robbery of widows and orphans; living under the same roof with their husbands' parents and sometimes with their brothers- and sisters-in-law as well—all that sort of thing the women of Algeria have grown to resent as a hateful imposition.

When you ask the children in a Constantine or an Algiers shanty-town what they want to be when they grow up, the little boys (like every little boy in Europe or America) talk about owning a super-car. But the little girls almost all want to be teachers—and not to marry. Well, what chance has the boy to own a car if he stays in his own country? As for the girl, she will be married before she is fifteen, quite likely against her will and quite likely to a pensioner old enough to be her grandfather.

"But it's all their own fault," you will hear some settlers say. "Why do they divorce their wives for the merest whim? Why do they tear the children away from their mothers so brutally? Why do they treat their wives so badly? Why do they have so many children? And if it's not their fault, it's the fault of their religion. In any case, it's not ours."

No, it is not their fault, nor that of the settlers, nor even that of Islam.[2] It is the fault of a certain social climate that is the direct consequence of the clash of their institutions with ours. *And it is no longer possible today to live in that social climate.*

The two million Moslems who are, economically

---

[2] Islam displays more toleration of birth-control than does the Catholic Church, and in the seventh century, when the Koran was written, the position enjoyed by women in Moslem and in Christian countries was the same.

speaking, Europeans may be well off compared with their co-religionists, but that only makes them more sensitive to the hundred and one indignities that the social disintegration of their country holds in store for them. As there has to be some scapegoat for all these big tragedies and little irritations, they blame everything on "the settlers" or on "colonialism." Neither, of course, is absolutely innocent or completely guilty.

Following a well-established pattern, the leaders of the present revolution were drawn from a group that was economically privileged but socially and politically slighted.[3] Thus, if they succeed, some of them will be

---

[3] Up to 1954 there were two groups of electors in Algeria, the First and Second Colleges, and each College returned the same number of representatives. The Second College comprised the majority of the Moslem electors; the First College was composed of the European-born electors, the Algerian Jewish electors, and certain classes of Moslem electors, the ex-servicemen in particular. The latest electoral register showed that the First College numbered 570,000 electors (roughly corresponding to a population of 1,250,000 non-Moslems and 350,000 Moslems), whereas the Second College (with 1,450,000 electors) was supposed to represent the great bulk of the Moslem population—that is, more than 8,000,000 people. It is easy to see that the vote of an elector belonging

among the people who will try to emigrate (probably to France) in order to escape from the disaster they will have helped to bring about. Naturally, that is a prospect which can hardly appeal to a Frenchman, but you have to expect that sort of nonsense when you let an abnormal situation take root in a country. And, after all, it is quite as natural as, and no sillier than, the tricks of the same sort which have been played there the other way around by the minority that uses the name of France. In both cases, they score a direct hit on their own heads with the boomerang they have aimed at "the guy over there."

If one in every three human beings in Algeria is, economically speaking, a European, what are the two others?

They are people who do not enjoy a single one of the solid benefits of our civilization, but who nevertheless are far better acquainted with them, want them far more, and are consequently far better fitted to use them than the inhabitants of any of the other countries of Africa or Asia.

International financiers should reflect a little on

---

to the First College counted for at least six times as much as that of an elector of the Second College.

this cruel contrast. In other places, if you stuff the wallets of a handful of petty tyrants, you can work the richest oilfields in the world with comparatively little to worry about. You cannot in Algeria. And from that point of view, one really can say that "Algeria is France," for I will make bold to assert that until every single Algerian is getting the minimum French standard of living, it will be impossible to invest a penny of capital in the country with any safety. Independence will not improve a thing—in fact, I should say the other way around—because all the grievances and the frustrations that are tormenting the men of Algeria are somehow or other mixed up with the political demand for independence. What does independence mean to the fighting *fellagha?* "It'll be the end of the bad times," they say, and they mean work, schools, houses, clean and hard-working wives, money, land, and bread. What, they're not out for an Arab state? you will ask. Yes, naturally; they want an Arab state that will provide all that. And if it fails to, the new state had better watch its step, for that is what the men are fighting for, with set teeth and angry hearts.

These facts are worth the reflection, too, of the

nationalist leaders and of the statesmen of Algeria's neighbors.

"All-that-France-has-done-in-Algeria" (the hospitals, the roads, the port facilities, the big towns, the beginnings of an industry, and a quarter of the schools that are needed) and "All-that-France-hasn't-done-in-Algeria" (the remaining three quarters of the necessary schools, other industries, and an agricultural plan with the agrarian reform and the technical experts it will call for) form together a sort of explosive compound, to the destructive force of which our accomplishments contribute no less powerfully than our misdeeds.

And now that the good and the evil that we have done have fused to produce one of the most terrifying time-bombs in the world, quite a number of Frenchmen, it must be admitted, cherish the daydream of leaving Algeria and the Algerians to sort out their own problems as best they can. Well, we undertook to solve those problems, and they are still soluble—at an enormous effort, but not one beyond our means. Without our aid, whatever happens, they will never be solved.

VII

The Link between France and Algeria Is Not a Political Fiction

FRANCE AND ALGERIA are indeed linked today by a two-way flow of emigrants that commits both sides, irrespective of what they may feel. There is the old stream of emigration, the "settlers" coming from Europe, and its modern counterpart, the emigration of Moslem workers to France.

These two opposite streams of migration both bear responsibility for the evolution of Algeria, and to that extent both are contributing to the present crisis. But they both also represent a financial stimulant that partially offsets (and therefore obscures) an economic situation which has become extremely precarious.

These 400,000 Algerian workers are known to every Frenchman by sight, but I have met well-meaning people who still have no idea why they come to France. Some of these people are convinced that the Algerians have been enticed over here in spite of themselves by crooked employers who then do not employ them. Others think that the immigrants come simply out of a taste for travel, or to hold up late-evening strollers on deserted suburban roads.

In fact, this mass emigration of several hundred thousand men represents several hundred thousand acts of courage and initiative, and several hundred thousand acts of courage and devotion to a starving family. They are a living proof that the Algerian people are neither passive nor fatalistic, but possess the will to shape a better existence for themselves and the capacity to do so. Just try to imagine the daring these men needed to launch out into the unknown when many of them had never seen an automobile or a railway, or even a water tap or a staircase. I knew two men who, three years apart, were the first men from their respective tribes (none of whose members spoke French) to strike out on their own. I could gauge the risk they were taking, for they had to sell their poor belongings and part with their land, and all this without having a shred of a contract or any promise of one, or even knowing where to go to look for work. And what kind of work, anyway? Naturally, they did not know any trade, and, as I have told you, they understood no French. They did not take my advice, and they left. It was they who were right, for a man must live.

French industry thus employs today 400,000 Algerian workers and directly supports—in Algeria itself—about two million people. We know from the post office the figures of the regular remittances sent by these new settlers: three years ago they were running at the rate of thirty-five billion francs a year, but they are increasing yearly and must now be between forty and forty-five billion. In addition to the direct effects of this transfusion of money and the current of economic activity it sets up through the purchases made by the recipients of the remittances—purchases that provide a living for shops, industries, and farms—there are other and less expected repercussions. Many an Algerian peasant leaving for France had a little plot of land that was no longer enough to keep his family alive; before leaving, he transferred it to a relation on a share-cropping basis. This procedure has become so frequent in the areas from which men are emigrating to France that the old systems of farm tenancy have been transformed within less than ten years, and the tenant now gets half the crop instead of one fifth. Moreover, the relation who could not live off his own plot can keep going now that it has been enlarged in this way. Maybe, then, we should double the figure for people who are being kept by the courage of the voluntary exiles; maybe we should put it at three or even at four million. Three or four million hands are thus stretched out to us, three or four million chains bind them and bind us too.

But while the current of this new migration is flowing toward Europe, the previous current has left its deposits, the descendants of the men who thought they had conquered Africa: a million and a half hostages, a million and a half other chains that bind France to Algeria or, if you wish, Algeria to France.

There are people who suggest that these hostages should be resettled in the French villages which are being drained by rural depopulation, and would confine our development work and our capital investment to the home country for the future. Financial circles are fond of quoting the examples of Holland—which has done so well since it lost the Dutch East Indies—

and of Germany, whose enormous economic progress has been stimulated by the absence of colonial possessions.

Other people talk of parking the "settlers" in a "reservation," like those for Indians in the United States, but a reservation that would be kept for them and defended by them. Beyond its borders, as independent as you please, would be left to pullulate a destitution of which no Algerian has any idea: the poverty of the loaf-divided-in-five and then in six, until it came to the loaf-divided-in-ten of the concentration camps, and finally to the day when there was no bread at all. . . . This second solution is sometimes referred to as "the Palestinian solution," but it might just as well be called "the Mau-Mau solution." For that is the solution the British adopted in Kenya, a solid frontier that divides a prosperous minority from a starving majority—until the inevitable day when the frontier gives way. When that happens, the only solution possible is that imposed by the strongest—whether in firepower or in numbers—for there is no longer a question of any equitable solution.

Should we withdraw to France, or set up a European reservation in Algeria? The first course means the complete destruction of the country's economic structure; the second, that it would deliberately be left to atrophy. In either case, we should be abandoning to their fate a people who, after having put up with (and suffered from) the European system, are now incapable of doing without it. It would spell the death of the local industry, which may employ no more than 100,000 Moslem workers, but which directly supports more than half a million people, who themselves give employment to tradespeople ranging from the baker to the radio and even the motorcycle dealer, taking in the local chain store and the bus company on the way—in a word, to all the activities that flourish around families that have a regular paycheck coming in. It would mean the ruin of the railways, the post office, the hotel industry, the garages, the upkeep of the roads, everything that at the start tended to harm the local population (in the sense that it precipitated their evolution), but which *today, when that evolution is halfway to accomplishment,* they are coming to regard as indispensable.

While these disastrous plans are being hatched out here, the Algerian nationalists are not sitting with their hands folded: they are championing plans the mildest of which would involve its fair share of catastrophes. But that is the way things are: anything that either side does in the country now is doomed in advance *unless the plan allows it to catch up culturally, economically, and socially with the advanced countries*, for that today is an absolute must for Algeria. The necessity for such a transformation arises not from any preconceived opinion, but from the density of Algeria's population, the state of the country's development, and its natural resources, and I will remind you how this balance sheet reads. Algeria has nine million inhabitants. As an archaic rural country, it could feed two million (which was the approximate figure of its population in 1830, though this may be exaggerated, as in a country of nomads there is a tendency to count the same people twice). Thus, it would have seven million inhabitants to get rid of. As a prosperous industrial country, on the other hand, it would be underpopulated.

"Here's the place for you, agronomists, builders, engineers, and every sort of technician there is," we might well say. "There's room and to spare for you in an Algeria that plays to win." But in an Algeria that throws its hand in, three inhabitants in every four will have to emigrate or die.

The chief demand of the F.L.N., the nationalist party that seems at the moment to command the most support, is not independence but the formation of a North African Union. The members of this Union would be the independent states of Tunisia and Morocco, and an Algeria whose right to opt for or against independence would have been recognized in advance. Such a Union could then link up with France. Many French politicians—particularly financiers—support this solution, as do the Tunisian and Moroccan governments.

Now, the population of Morocco today is just over seven million and that of Tunisia just under three million, which means that in any sort of association of the three countries the dominant partner could only be Algeria. Algeria has as many inhabitants as the two others combined, her central position strengthens her claim to leadership of her neighbors, and the collective temper of her people is extremely assertive and little inclined to take second place.

The Moroccans are monarchists and traditionalists,

the Algerians proletarians and republicans, so the connection seems to present some danger to the former, if only from a dynastic point of view. What is more, Morocco has a long way to go before she reaches the critical population density, and she has a chance of becoming a genuinely independent country. But she will never achieve it if she has this millstone of an Algeria around her neck.

As for Tunisia, her present stability is a miracle, due to a good government and to the fact that her institutions are more modern and sounder than those of Algeria and Morocco. But that stability is extremely precarious, and would founder at the first serious shock. And she could hardly hope to escape shocks as a member of the ill-balanced partnership that is envisaged.

The risk cuts both ways, for there would be a grave danger to the Algerian proletariat if it found itself in competition on the French labor market with the proletariats of Morocco and Tunisia.

Our relations with Morocco and Tunisia bear no sort of likeness to those we have with Algeria; the latter are, anyway, of a type unique in the world. The connections we have with Morocco and Tunisia, on the other hand, are of a kind that has become standard, and if we compare them with our ties (similar, but with the roles reversed) to our American allies, we may begin to understand the ill-feeling toward us which is sometimes displayed in Tunis and Rabat. And, for that matter, the ill-temper with which Washington sometimes requites our own—for, as we are ourselves both a "satellite" and the center of a satellite system, we are in the best position to appreciate both sides of the question.

In short, financial experts tell us that France's alliance with Tunisia costs her an annual drain of about 25 billion francs (including the balance of trade), while our friendship with Morocco runs us into 40 billion francs a year, or perhaps a little more. But at that price, if we have the patience to wait a little while, we can hope to forge links of friendship with both countries which will benefit them as much as they will us. Negotiations and dealings, differences and reconciliations, loans or gifts, all go on at the Ministerial level; the average Frenchman or Moroccan or Tunisian has nothing to do with them, and if he does stick his finger into the pie, he will only mess things up. It is, to be quite precise, none of his affair.

ALGERIA

One fine day, let us hope, the three peoples will wake up to find themselves allies, and their alliance—like the Entente Cordiale—will have been quietly brought into existence by a handful of officials and a few statesmen who were just doing their duty.

The worst thing that can happen—a breach in Franco-Tunisian or Franco-Moroccan relations—will do no harm to anything but the state budgets of Tunisia and Morocco. Only indirectly will the private budgets of the individual Tunisians or Moroccans feel its effects, through the economic, social, and possibly political crisis that may result from the failure to meet civil-service and army pay, the stoppage of public works, and bankruptcy.

However, it is not just Ministries and civil servants who bind and loose the connections between France and Algeria. Hundreds of thousands of people from the two countries have, without knowing what they were doing, forged the links in the chain across the Mediterranean that holds us. That explains the seriousness and the irrevocable nature of the relations which constrain us *on both sides*, whether we want it or not.

Suppose tomorrow an independent Algeria joins

this North African Union that so many people of different opinions are urging, along with Tunisia and Morocco; suppose the institution is inaugurated without any immediate catastrophe, that the Union spontaneously enters into a wholehearted alliance with France, and that the French government—in return for certain economic concessions—agrees to pay the Algerian government the annual hundred billion francs without which it could not exist: of late we have been providing Algeria with 150 billion francs. Everything would appear to be going swimmingly. The Algerian Moslems would obviously, it stands to reason, cease to hold French nationality, but as that is exactly what they are asking for (or, rather, what is being asked for in their name), they would have got what they wanted. And we should have been discharged, it would seem, from a very onerous responsibility.

French citizenship and everything that goes with it (free education, social insurance, and other advantages) has so far only brought French Moslems benefits that they have been unable to appreciate, for their sole measuring-rod is our own economic standards, which are statistically higher than theirs. Moreover, the "special status" of Algeria has given the various departments a handle for paring these benefits down. Naturally, Moslem Algerians have a right to family allowances—but not at the same rates as in France. Of course social insurance is open to them—but they must know the rights it entitles them to and the method of claiming these, and that means they must have been to school. There is not the slightest bar to their enjoying compulsory elementary education—as long as there is a teacher in their village. Pensions for the blind are open to them, too—but at a different rate, and so forth.

While one set of honest French officials (sticklers for justice and humanity) was pulling one way, another set of no less honest civil servants (enthusiasts for sound finances and balanced budgets) was pulling, with no less conviction, in the other. Both sides could draw equally valid arguments from the legal position of Algeria, for "Algeria was France," but at the same time it was not completely France. When you add to all this the peculiar racial-economic-religious complex that surrounds Algeria, plus a bunch of powerful and well-organized private interests, you will understand how the best of intentions can come to nothing, and why one can regard only with the deepest suspicion any sort of definition of the phrase used by politicians who do not want to commit themselves to recognizing Algerian autonomy: "the personality of Algeria." Knowing as I do the reflexes that are set up in poor and uneducated countries, I can guess only too well the practical translation of the future definition: "Personality of the French worker: 4,000 calories. Personality of the autonomous Algerian: 2,000."

In the plan the Algerian nationalists put forward, the Algerian worker will not even preserve the privileged position he enjoys today, for he will be on the same footing in his relations with us as the Moroccans and Tunisians, who will probably soon be joined by the citizens of other allied countries of Europe and Africa. Now, I am unfortunately in a position to state that on the French labor market the Moroccan worker, who is healthier and better disciplined, beats the Algerian hollow, while Italian builders and Belgian and Polish miners are at a premium. The only reason why so many Algerians are working in France is that there is no legal way of keeping them out; the French identity cards which they hold, and which their foreign rivals do not, act as a measure of protection in their favor. If they lost that trump, only the skilled and steady workers would be able to visit their families with the assurance—thanks to a contract—of being able to get back to France again. The rest of them—three quarters, probably, and more later—would be finished. The prospect is an attractive one to many French employers. That is quite natural. The kind of employee they want is the man who is best at his work, not the man who needs a job most. But it is also natural that the more a man needs work, the less good he is likely to be as a worker. If some groups of Algerians have such a low productivity, the reason is that they are suffering from malnutrition. But it is precisely because they do not have enough to eat that they leave their families and their home country.

A few figures will suffice to show just how much of a practical advantage the French identity card is. Morocco and Tunisia have between them a population of about ten million, much the same as Algeria's. Both of them suffer from considerable unemployment. Yet the latest statistics show that they have only 30,000 workers in France, as compared to nearly 400,000 Algerians. That means that *a French identity card gives an unskilled worker, at any rate, a ten-times-*

better chance of finding a job in France[1]—which is understandable, once one knows the way in which "general laborers" are taken on.

I have often heard young Algerian students explaining that, granted American (or Soviet) aid, Algeria could do without France. But if you have followed what has gone before, you will understand that the problem confronting Algeria is a problem of *wages*—a problem that is, for the moment, insoluble within the limits of Algeria (even with unlimited capital) but perfectly capable of solution in a Franco-Algerian set-up, provided that adequate capital and sufficient experts were available.

People talk a great deal about the "fabulous mineral wealth" of the Sahara. Probably it does exist,

---

[1] There are people in France who would be delighted to be able to get rid of a certain Algerian underworld to which they attribute many more crimes than its members in fact commit: statistically, the percentage of offenders among the two communities is much the same. What I am maintaining is that in the process of ridding ourselves of a few real undesirables, we should be taking the bread from the mouths of hundreds of thousands of families, *for I do not know of a single Algerian—though I am told they do exist—who has come to France with a job waiting for him.* It is only after they are here that they find work.

for there is something everywhere, and a thousand times more potential in a billion acres than in a million acres. But even if the natural resources are there, can they be exploited?

If the world were a free-trade world, it would not enter anyone's head to industrialize the Sahara for a good half-century, because a pound of iron or a gallon of oil from the Sahara would inevitably cost much more than the iron of the Ruhr or the oil of the Middle East. If the world were a peaceful place, the big international companies would have an obvious interest in preventing competitors from opening up new mines and oil wells even at a loss, and an equal interest in preventing their own profits from being cut by the addition of new fields to those which they already control *and which are sufficient for the needs of the world as it is.* It has even been suggested that some of them might like to see the present state of insecurity in North Africa go on indefinitely. But the world is neither a free-trade world nor a peaceful one. So if the companies take a broad view and gauge the danger of the stormclouds that are now piling up in the skies of Asia and Africa, they may well try to spread their risks, so as to set off against one another the various national appetites that are inevitably inordinate, inevitably doomed to disappointment, and inevitably destructive.

Algeria's appetite happens to be both more inordinate and more destructive than that of the other unadapted peoples. As against that, the job of turning it into an adapted country would be well within the range of possibility, *because it is already half adapted. The transformation is possible physically, financially, and psychologically.*

One day even financiers will understand that the only real wealth of a country is the people living there. With them, anything can be done; against them, thank heavens, nothing—or, anyway, nothing sound and durable.

Should we not let the Algerians in on the profits of the "Sahara business"? It would be an equitable, satisfactory, and forward-looking thing to do. But the fact is that the unfortunate people will have every chance of dying of hunger ten times over before the "Sahara business" begins to pay its way, and will therefore have ample leisure to destroy their tomorrow's daily bread because they have not got today's—to eat their seed corn while waiting for the sowing, like my luckless friends of the Aurès. What is more, if one is to profit from a situation, one must be in a position to seize one's chance, and the poor and uneducated man is ringed around with a sort of magic circle which is all but impassable, and which makes it impossible to do this. Give him money,[2] and he will not get it; provide him with sound laws, and they will turn out to harm him; give him capable civil servants, and they will be snowed under by crooks. In other words, *it is impossible to look after a people that is not capable of looking after itself.* That is one of the reasons for the bankruptcy of colonialism, and it will also be responsible for the bankruptcies that are pending in the "Pauper World." Characteristic of the position is the example of Saudi Arabia, which has the world's lowest standard of liv-

---

[2] Talking of the appalling shortage of capital for development in Poland, a high Polish official said recently: "What is more, forty per cent of what is invested is pure stupidity, waste, or corruption." There are the same stupidity, waste, and corruption in all the countries where capital is insufficient—that is, in all the underdeveloped countries. Marxist and capitalist governments can shake hands over this: one is no better than the other.

ing along with the richest oilfields in the world, in full production.

If the Algerians are to have a share in the "Sahara business," they must first be let in on the profits of the "France business." For our part, we should realize that we shall be able to exploit the Sahara only on condition that we do not exploit the Sahara's population. And to do that, we ourselves should help them to defend themselves against the harmfulness of our institutions—though this harmfulness is purely conditional, like the harmfulness of fresh air for a tadpole that has not changed into a frog in time.

The Sahara holds out for us a chance of real independence—the loss of which we have been in a position to appreciate these last few months—but it means even more. It will make demands on our inventiveness, our capacity to grow, to develop, to take a chance, to put our shoulders to the wheel. If all this is so, we must pay the price *before we start.* If we give, we shall receive. But we must remember, too, that we have shouted at the top of our voices that "Algeria is French." We must not forget that for more than a century Algerians have been shedding their blood in our wars. If the words *honor* and *humanity* mean anything, we should realize that they put us under an obligation.

Supposing Algeria were to attain autonomy: to provide it with no more than the equivalent of the little remittances of ten thousand, fifteen thousand, and twenty thousand francs which are still coming from France (and which two million people depend on every month to be able to eat) would call for local industries capable of offering employment to 400,000 extra laborers. This in turn would require rather more than *two billion francs' worth of capital, ten years of social tranquillity, and very large and easily workable natural resources.* Now, any expectation of social tranquillity in such conditions is a pure delusion. The mineral resources of the Sahara will be expensive and difficult to work, political insecurity will help to slow down the investment of capital, the capital will in any case be insufficient to stave off the Algerian explosion, and the explosion will scare away overnight whatever funds are being invested.

France is the only country that has an interest in spending large sums of money on the development of the Sahara's mineral resources. They will show very little profit to start with, and their costs will in any case be higher than those of the American and Middle Eastern oilfields—but they will help us cut down our expenditure of foreign currencies. If someone else is to step into France's shoes in Algeria, therefore, millions of people will have to reconcile themselves to dying of hunger so as not to frighten away the capital that will provide their country—not for ten years, and not for certain even then—with the equivalent of the workers' earnings which the country is getting today *and which even now are inadequate.* Obviously that is too much to expect; there is not a people in the world which could stomach such a catastrophic fall in a standard of living already below the minimum. The result would be an explosion, and the collapse of the second pillar of the country's economy—that which is now provided by the European-born minority of the population.

What could an independent Algerian government do to get out of such a mess? You may say it could protect the settlers so as to prevent them from leaving, as has happened in Morocco. They would leave, all the same, for no Algerian government would be strong enough to protect them, and they would be in deadly peril—far more than in Morocco. In trying to protect them, the Algerian government would only risk losing its only trump card—the indispensable agrarian reform. In not trying to protect them, it would be opening the way to the second wave of the economic breakdown, which would engulf the country.

If the unhappy people are today sustained over the mouth of hell, they owe it to two pillars, and two pillars alone: to the economic and administrative framework manned by the ethnic minority who are called colonial, and to the industrial system of France. It may be true that not all the Moslems of Algeria are dependent exclusively and directly for their living on one of these two pillars. But, firstly, nearly all those who live a normal life owe almost the whole of their income to one of these pillars, and, secondly, practically all the others—those who live in want—get from one or the other of them, often indirectly, at least part of their income. But let there be no mistake: that part is not sufficient for the upkeep of a car, or the cost of a holiday, or even the purchase of necessary clothing or the cost of eating a little better. Supposing the French industrial system contributes three twelfths, four twelfths, or eight twelfths of a family's income, that means that without it the family would have to go without eating for three months, four months, or eight months of the year. That is the reason why there can be no question of dividing up or reducing the individual income of this class of Algerians. The money that is coming into each household now must continue coming in, *and continue without interruption and without reduction* on pain of a catastrophe. It is also the reason why, by what only seems a paradox to a stranger's eyes, the shock of a breach with France would almost certainly hit the small incomes more severely than the relatively well-to-do class, despite the fact that the French contribution to the former is extremely small and to the latter relatively large. The difference is that the former can neither cut their expenses nor find other jobs, whereas the latter, with money or professional qualifications behind them, are adapted people who even in bad times would be able to make shift at home and who, if the worst came to the worst, would be able to pick up and find jobs elsewhere.

Meanwhile, here in France 400,000 families have had to resign themselves to seeing their sons leave for Algeria, where some of them have been killed. Killed by whom? you will ask. By an Algerian, obviously. And who has taken the missing son's place at the factory or the workshop? An Algerian, too. You will admit that it is a bit hard.

All the same, the ordinary people are putting up with the situation, putting up with it better than we had any right to hope. With some of them, the motive has been traditional sympathy for the underdog; with others, the fact that they have always felt that Algeria was France and therefore dreaded the prospect of a separation between the two as they would an amputation. For both, the present war is a civil war, a fratricidal struggle—which naturally does not prevent their hurling insults at each other.

It must be admitted that the strain is felt on both sides, and that the people of Algeria, caught as they are in a vice between the *fellagha* and the government forces, are standing up with incredible patience under an ordeal that is as appalling morally as it is physically. They are also displaying a no less incredible ambiguity in their feelings—for if they did not protect the settlers (I mean the farmers among them), do you think there would be any European farmers left?

It seems only normal that there should be some

hatred felt for us among the Algerians, and there are outrages every day which testify to it. The same hatred exists the other way around, and I have been distressed more than once to run into it. What is more, there are today men on both sides who run amuck and fling themselves blindly into violence for its own sake. In looking back over the past, one can also find actions and writings that bear witness to obtuseness or ill-feeling. But almost as often, today as in the years gone by, it is the opposite attitude that stands out, in both communities alike: an avid curiosity about a new kind of human beings, a prepossession in their favor, delight at being able to live in the atmosphere they provide. Hardly a Frenchman who has lived in Algeria leaves it without homesickness. In the opposite camp, even among the nationalist leaders, you will find the same fascination the other way round.

How fragile all that seems in the face of this stupid, sanguinary, and interminable war, and of the prospects for the future which the war compels us to contemplate.

Other peoples apparently manage, without making any trouble, to live a life that varies between chronic malnutrition and the sort of famine which kills. But then they have never known anything else, and they have never had any occasion to hope. The Algerian people do have hope, and the real "Algerian war" has not begun—or not yet.

Conclusion

THE BANE of our century today is the economic and cultural collapse that afflicts unadapted peoples when they come into contact with industrial peoples. All the same, as long as there is a single colony left in the world, colonialism will have to shoulder the blame for the scourge that has followed in its wake: too many little local despots and too many financial groups have an interest in diverting to such a handy lightning-conductor the only too real popular aggressiveness with which they also will have to reckon one fine day. That means that to be a colonial power today is inevitably to be a scapegoat. The British, who have handed over power wherever they have been able to, have grasped that point.

Our turn has come to carry through the transformation that the times demand of us. If we had done it earlier, we should have saved a lot of blood, a lot of money, and also something that costs dear both in blood and in money and is called hatred. At any rate, we have finally got it into our heads that the colonial formula is as dead as a doornail now, and that a continuance of the *status quo* is no longer possible.

Is this enough? I do not think so, for our presence in our overseas possessions has had a profoundly disturbing effect on them, politically, socially, and economically.

Everywhere we went, we planked down a foreign administration—and the old local institutions became atrophied, while (under the influence of overpopulation and of the collapse of the traditional cultures and economies) the masses that they had once directed turned into a more complex society and multiplied inordinately. That means that the old African institutions are no longer capable of taking over from the colonial administration, and that the young countries will have to improvise—under the worst possible economic, social, political, and demographic conditions, and with inadequate and poorly trained staffs—a new administration and brand-new institutions. The task is a fantastic one.

We certainly did not think we had done such a bad job when we put down slavery or cannibalism, defended the sedentary peasants against the raiding nomads, stamped out epidemics and tribal wars, built bridges and roads and factories, looked after the children and taught them to read. But a social system is a coherent whole, and when you destroy what is bad in it, you weaken what is good. Between them, the men who oppressed and exploited these countries and those who loved them and gave up their lives to them sawed through the main beams that held up the hoary political edifice in which human beings had been living for thousands of years. Their collapse was probably inevitable. All the same, we should not forget that it was through us and with us that it happened, and we should beware lest by withdrawing our guardianship we do these peoples even more harm than we did when we imposed it on them:

Now good-by, I'm out of this deal.
Try to scrape along,
And put your shoulder to the wheel.

We shall have to devise political links flexible enough to be loosened without bloodshed, and also capable of being tightened, as the course of an experiment that has not yet started may require. The experiment of Eurafrica? you may ask. Maybe.

We shall have to disinter and put new life into old forms of social life capable of being adapted to democratic institutions. Coherent groups—vestiges of former tribes—still exist almost everywhere in Africa. It would be possible to consult them on the size and the frontiers of the unit they want to form; it would be possible to provide this unit with the flexible, liberal, and inexpensive set-up of our communes in France. Within the "tribe-commune" there would be peace, and that, after all, is something.

Between the "tribe-commune" and the authorities at the center we shall inevitably have to provide for intermediate units, which will represent a threat to the young state because they will have no natural basis. If they were direct emanations of the central government, there would be the danger both of its using them as an instrument for the exploitation and oppression of the people, and, conversely, of their threatening the unity of the country. Maybe the Swiss cantonal system would give the local inhabitants the best chance of looking after themselves and developing along lines that would be likely to suit them. Features that would be particularly useful to them are its electoral registration of citizens at their birthplace, and its allocation of responsibility for public assistance.

Economic links between our former colonies and ourselves will remain too. But I expect you will agree that economic tie-ups between countries of unequal development should be regarded with the utmost suspicion: they may be inevitable, but we should at least recognize the grave danger to which they expose the weaker partner. What is more, there is going to be some cutthroat competition in this field, and no one can be sure that the next figure in the dance will be the last.

All the same, these countries have the good luck to be sparsely populated. That means that they will profit from a stay of execution during which they can bring their traditions into harmony with the biological demands of world civilization—for the termination of the colonial relationship does not alter the inevitability of the contact between their civilizations and the industrial system. They will have to take care, and we shall have to take care with them, for arrangements that are arrived at by mutual agreement give no sort of guarantee against the unhappiest consequences. The American or British recipes of setting up an industrial complex in a theoretically free country are as inhuman, as tragic in their consequences, and therefore in the end as stupid and as costly as the colonialist recipe. *When you establish an industry or a single-crop economy in a country—whether the country is colonial or free is of little importance—you should start by putting the people of the country in a position to defend themselves against the system in which you are going to force them to live, and the first essential for that is for you to bear the costs of their adaptation.* In other words, you are only doing harm if you establish an industry in a country where the population has not attained the standard of industrial civilization as we have defined it: full political rights, universal education, and full employment. If you neglect these obligations, you will sooner or later have on your hands a tragic social collapse, for which the rich nations will bear the moral responsibility, not to mention the lost profits and the political and strategic difficulties, while the poor nation will be overwhelmed by an avalanche of calamities.

There is another link already in existence between France and a great part of Africa. It is an intellectual, a personal, and a potentially enduring link, and whether it shall be a beneficent one depends on us alone. The whole future of French West Africa, French Equatorial Africa, and Madagascar, all countries with no linguistic unity, may depend on their success or failure in finding a common "international language," and French is today in an excellent position to play this role. Not only will such a common language favor their political unity and their chance of profiting from the economic opportunities that are going to be offered to them: their very life depends on it. For though they may have been granted a stay of execution to adapt themselves to world civilization, it is no more than a stay, and they will be able to profit from it only if they have at their disposal a widely spoken modern language.

None of this is any help to Algeria. Algeria has long ago passed the moment when any stay of execution was possible. When did that happen? I should be inclined to place it between 1900 and 1920. Today the choice before Algeria is a choice between immediate conversion to an intensive industrial civilization, or a swift decline punctuated by sanguinary interludes.

The *sine qua non* for Algeria, in fact, amounts to eight or ten years of elementary education for every child, and a trade, a job, a good wage, modern social legislation, and a ballot that is not tampered with for every adult. In a word, everything that we have and the Algerians have not.

Would that be enough? Between certain archaic civilizations and our own, there exist such fundamental incompatibilities that, even if the inhabitants were offered the complete social outfit we have at our disposal, they would probably continue to turn up their noses at our system. Maybe that was the position of the American Indians, and possibly it was an even more important factor in their disappearance than the systematic destruction to which they were subjected. In the case of Algeria, however, these incompatibilities do not exist. I have been to Indian Reservations in America, and, compared with them, I find an Algiers shanty-town a cheerful sight, for there at least people are struggling and aspiring, planning and hoping. Give Algerians the means to live, and live they will.

There are indeed several indications that the social distortion in Algeria is in a sense less serious than that of other peoples who are still enjoying a peaceful existence. The two communities that make up the Algerian population may be separated by an enormous economic gap, but the corresponding social gap between them is of nothing like the same proportions. To check on that, you have only to notice with what facility men (and even groups of men) from the destitute class enter the prosperous class when a favorable opportunity makes it possible for them to do so. There is nothing inevitable about the Algerians' woes. Their social and economic decline is not written in the stars, and the ready-dug grave which is waiting for them, we and they have dug between us with our own hands. That makes it all the more heart-rending to follow the ups and downs of the present tragedy, in which everything is being done by all concerned to make those woes and that decline incurable.

On the French side, there are those who want to retain certain privileges and those who would like to be rid of a heavy financial burden. The first attitude is an outdated daydream: the second would doom Algeria irrevocably to the worst of fates. But though we in France may know far too little about the needs and aspirations of the Algerian masses, the nationalist leaders behave as if they knew equally little about the peremptory demands of their own followers and the reactions of the ordinary Frenchman. They do not realize, in the first place, the scale of the sacrifices that their country must make if it is merely to keep going—and "merely to keep going," in Algeria's case, means to stave off an appalling day of reckoning. They do not realize, either, that the Algerian workers in France would be only too easy to replace, and that they would have next to no chance of finding any work elsewhere. Above all, they regard as a success for them the fact that the majority of Frenchmen are fed up with the present war. There is nothing comforting about that, however, for the same attitude that balks at sending troops to Algeria will balk at providing the country with the billions and the experts it needs, and will deny Algerians access to our factories.

Now, as I see it, the crux of the whole problem is that Algeria is irretrievably lost unless it manages by hook or by crook to retain the exclusive right of entry to the French labor market which it now enjoys, a right that is not compatible, at least on the Franco-Algerian level, with a North African Union and perhaps not even with Eurafrica.[1] On top of this right, the country needs, as soon as possible, a minimum of 300,000 additional jobs, which, together with universal education and a reasonable measure of agrarian reform, would call for the investment of more than 2,000 billion francs of capital, spread over four or five years. This would come to approximately 400 billion francs a year, just about what the war is costing us now.

A high proportion of this enormous sum can only come from France, for it is needed for such un-

---

[1] On the other hand, from the only point of view that concerns us here (seeing that Algeria has enough to eat), one can conceive of a series of concentric circles whose center would be a Franco-Algerian Union, which could then enter as a unit into any other federation that could be thought of: North Africa, Eurafrica, or Eurafroamerica. The key point to remember is that if, within one of these federations, Algeria was to be on the same juridical footing in relation to us as another overpopulated and underdeveloped country, any hope of raising her to the industrial level would be killed stone dead.

secured investments as schools, the economic infrastructure of the country, and carefully planned agrarian reforms. If these investments are made, however, there is more than a possibility that private capital, French or foreign, may start to flow in. But a company would require a lot of courage to plank down a factory in a country where energy is dear, roads and bridges are few, skilled labor is scarce and expensive, lack of money has kept the people's consumption low, and where, one fine morning, just because of all that, the local population may burn the factory down.

In 1956, Algerian education cost France 29.8 billion francs. This is not enough, because it gives Algeria no chance of catching up on her backwardness in relation to us in this field. If we want to even up the average cultural standards in the two countries, we shall have to increase the Algerian education estimates to 50 billion francs a year.[2] By paying this

---

[2] Some 50 billion francs, spread over five years, for fundamental education; in the suburbs and the countryside, this will come before the elementary school, but the curricula of the two will have to be co-ordinated. The same sum for various forms of vocational training: normal schools, agricultural colleges, and other kinds of technical training. Finally, over the

price, we would provide the conditions for prosperity, progress, and freedom too, for that matter—for to the poor and ignorant man, freedom is a mere mirage. The resuscitation of Algerian rural society,[3] within

---

five following years, 100 billion francs to complete the elementary-school installations.

[3] The present position of the Algerian peasantry is, as I see it, the biggest threat to any solution.

In the Berber-speaking areas, the land is divided on the death of the owner, and you can just imagine a fig tree divided among several families. In the Arab-speaking areas, it remains the joint property of the heirs, and nobody knows to whom any piece of land really belongs. That is why working farmers have stopped trying to plant trees or even to put fertilizer on their little lots, for the next year may see the reappearance of a couple of dozen cousins, who will resume their shares. This breaking up of property is carried out to such an extent that it has resulted in uncertainty as to rights, and thus forms the biggest obstacle to the improvement of agricultural techniques and yields.

If this obstacle is to be removed, the first essential is to provide the farmer with an inducement to farm well, which means, to start with, that he has to be given secure possession of his property. That is quite a proposition, for it necessitates making a survey, checking off all the properties, and carrying out a judicious reform of the existing legislation. And this in turn implies the availability of an army of experts with a good knowledge of existing rights and a capacity for administering and explaining the new laws, and also for deciding how large a property must be to provide a *normal living for a family*

its own traditional framework, is also capable of realization. It calls for no more than three factors: money, unoccupied land, and a lot of experts—the last being by far the most necessary element and the rarest. If these three factors were available, the pro-

---

(would it be 30 acres, 45 acres, or 60 acres?) and then identifying and protecting those which reached or exceeded this size. The administration must then be able to go to the owners of the substandard properties with an offer to buy or exchange their plots, and to resettle them, as opportunities occur, on land bought back from settlers or reclaimed from the desert; failing this, it must be in a position to teach them a trade and find them jobs in industry. Finally, there would come the piecing together of the smaller properties, a substantial increase in yields, the introduction of new crops and fertilizers, the setting up of co-operatives, and the inspection of markets—the way to all this being paved by serried ranks of schoolteachers.

Faced with a situation like this, many people (particularly agricultural experts) feel that a system such as the Soviet *kolkhozes* or the *kibbutzim* of Israel would call for less effort. I feel, on the contrary, that unless a government has at its disposal a formidable apparatus of police and prisons, and is reconciled to using this kind of strength pitilessly for years, it ought not to force on a peasant population the clean sweep of their previous institutions which such a system implies. Again, the example of Israel is hardly pertinent, as there the population is one of emigrants, who thus had no tradition of landholding.

gram could be set in motion by merely requiring every graduate of the French schools of agriculture and administration to do a compulsory two years of service in Algeria—naturally with a fair compensation.

The third condition for the salvation of Algeria, the provision of an additional 300,000 industrial jobs on top of the 50,000 that the Algerians already hold in their home country, is also within our reach. We have only to combine an intensive development of the Sahara with the maintenance of the privileged position that Algerians enjoy in France as against foreign competition.[4] For they would quite certainly lose that privileged position overnight if they lost their French identity cards.

None of these three conditions is optional. There must be 2,000 billion francs' worth of capital invest-

---

[4] People who are not familiar with the conditions of hiring where laborers are concerned may fancy that the question could be settled by intergovernmental contracts. But no sort of contract would be applicable to the fluid and completely unskilled mass that the Algerian workers form when they land in France. Moreover, one would be leaving out of account the extremely ambiguous feelings of the ordinary Frenchman if one imagined that a preferential attitude could survive a revision of our political links with Algeria.

ments in Algeria within five years; two years of compulsory service there for the graduates of certain of our French higher schools; and the maintenance of the Algerians' exclusive right of entry to our factories. If we are prepared to pay this price—and nothing less will do—then we shall be able to reverse the current. We shall be able to prevent an entire people from drifting on toward inevitable doom at a speed that might well increase violently, and finally to steer them toward that constant and practically limitless improvement of the general conditions of living which is the lot of the fortunate countries.

Can this program be reconciled with a federal arrangement? Anyone who knows France is likely to agree that it will be difficult. Yet it is more than probable that *if political concessions were accompanied by a precise and coherent development plan,* they would result, not in a secession of Algeria from France, but, on the contrary, in a consolidation of the unity of the two economies and therefore of the two political systems. On the other hand, if the political situation were to lead France to make a clean break in the ties between Algeria and herself, the whole program might blow up; there would be little likelihood of our agreeing to the necessary financial sacrifices—which would be no more than what the war is costing, though they would run to about three times what peace used to cost. Probably we should go on paying Algeria the usual little allowance, but it would be sheer waste, for the payment would serve no purpose but to gorge a set of sharks, pending the inevitable and incredibly sanguinary explosion.

If, on the other hand, we Frenchmen and Algerians did succeed one day in coming to an agreement and woke up to find ourselves coequal members of an imposing political unit, stretching over an enormous area, with natural resources no less complementary than diversified, we should form a firm foundation for a great system of freely negotiated alliances with the other peoples of Africa. We hear a lot of talk of such alliances, but they cannot be translated into reality today because the geographical keystone of the entire set-up is the great festering ulcer that Algeria has become.

Maybe if that Franco-Algerian dream came true we could put at the disposal of other nations the experience the two of us had gained together, by throwing ourselves into that colossal undertaking of the "Protection and Rescue of Peoples" whose broad lines I have just sketched out for you. And possibly our country, which has been one of the last to realize the bankruptcy of colonialism, may find herself taking the lead in the huge and enormously difficult rescue operation that is called for. Maybe she will be able finally to offer her companion peoples something better than ruin and decay.

You must not imagine, because I have confined myself to discussing the tragic problem of food, that I attach no importance to ancestral traditions, rituals, beliefs, and the mother tongue. But historical experience has taught us that the intellectual contributions two communities make to each other are never so great as when the contacts between them are closest: it is obvious what France owes to her religious minorities. It is because I know, value, and respect the moral and religious heritage of Algeria and appreciate the intellectual eagerness with which the young people are scanning the future that I feel certain of the mutual contributions they can expect from us and we from them. What have they to gain from reaching an understanding with us? Nothing less than a man's place in the world for themselves and a happy and honorable future for their children, instead of the terrifying decline that is lying in wait for them—a decline that will be economic to start with, then social, and then biological. By which time it will probably be beyond all hope of curing.

As for those famous deposits of this or that mineral, they are the prize that will be awarded to the Franco-Algerian Union, on top of everything else, if it manages to see the light of day. If it does not, the famous deposits will not be worth much, believe me. Even the big international companies may find they have burned their fingers by risking money on them.

Maybe this is asking a lot of us, maybe it is asking a lot of the Algerian intelligentsia, but if nobody on either side can or will make any concessions, then let us hurry up and make room in France for whomever we want to save in Algeria, whatever their race or their religion may be. The Algerian boat has ceased to be seaworthy, and there is no time to lose before the final wreck. But the disaster could have been avoided, and perhaps it still can.

ALGERIA

A NOTE ABOUT THE AUTHOR

GERMAINE TILLION, specialist on Algerian sociology, is Directeur d'Etudes at L'Ecole Pratique des Hautes Etudes (Sorbonne) (Social Science Department) and teaches the course "*Ethnographie du Maghreb.*"

Mlle Tillion spent the years from 1934 to 1940 in Algeria on scientific missions. From 1940 to 1942 she was the chief of a Resistance network, and then underwent three years of imprisonment when she was condemned to death on five counts. She wrote a history of the Second World War, and since 1954 has made several more extensive trips to the Aurès Mountains, the birthplace of the present rebellion.

Germaine Tillion has been awarded the *Rosette d'officier de la Légion d'honneur*, the *Croix de guerre*, and the *Rosette d'officier* for her Resistance work; and her studies of the Algerian people, as anthropologist and sociologist, have greatly influenced French opinion.

A NOTE ON THE TYPE

This book is set in Electra, a Linotype face designed by W. A. Dwiggins (1880–1956), who was responsible for so much that is good in contemporary book design. Although much of his early work was in advertising and he was the author of the standard volume *Layout in Advertising,* Mr. Dwiggins later devoted his prolific talents to book typography and type design, and worked with great distinction in both fields. In addition to his designs for Electra, he created the Metro, Caledonia, and Eldorado series of type faces, as well as a number of experimental cuttings that have never been issued commercially.

Electra cannot be classified as either modern or old-style. It is not based on any historical model, nor does it echo a particular period or style. It avoids the extreme contrast between thick and thin elements which marks most modern faces, and attempts to give a feeling of fluidity, power, and speed.

This book was composed, printed, and bound by H. WOLFF, New York. The paper was manufactured by P. H. GLATFELTER COMPANY, Spring Grove, Penn. Typography by GUY FLEMING. Binding based on an original design by GEORGE SALTER.